THIS BOOK BELONGS TO

_____

FOR THE KIDS WHO DREAM

ISBN: 9798894582009

LONG AGO, IN A PEACEFUL VILLAGE NESTLED AT THE FOOT OF A MISTY MOUNTAIN, THERE LIVED A WISE MONK NAMED BROTHER KAI. HE WAS KNOWN FAR AND WIDE FOR HIS CALM SPIRIT AND KIND HEART.

ONE DAY, VILLAGERS CAME RUSHING TO THE MONASTERY, THEIR FACES PALE WITH FEAR. "BROTHER KAI, HELP US!" THEY CRIED. "A STRANGE MIRROR HAS APPEARED IN THE FOREST. THOSE WHO LOOK INTO IT ARE NEVER SEEN AGAIN!"

KAI LISTENED CAREFULLY. HE NODDED, UNDERSTANDING THE URGENCY. "FEAR NOT," HE SAID, "I WILL FIND THIS MIRROR AND UNCOVER ITS SECRET."

AS THE SUN ROSE THE NEXT MORNING, BROTHER KAI VENTURED INTO THE DENSE FOREST. BIRDS CHIRPED AND LEAVES RUSTLED, BUT AN UNEASY SILENCE SOON ENVELOPED THE AIR.

DEEP WITHIN THE FOREST, HE FOUND IT—A TALL, GLEAMING MIRROR STANDING ALONE. ITS SURFACE SHIMMERED UNNATURALLY, AS IF ALIVE.

KAI APPROACHED CAUTIOUSLY. AS HE PEERED INTO THE MIRROR, HE SAW HIS OWN REFLECTION TWIST AND CHANGE. SUDDENLY, IT REACHED OUT AND PULLED HIM IN!

KAI FOUND HIMSELF IN A STRANGE, SHADOWY WORLD. AROUND HIM, VILLAGERS WANDERED, TRAPPED AND FRIGHTENED. "BROTHER KAI!" THEY CALLED. "HELP US!"

BEFORE HE COULD RESPOND, A CHILLING LAUGH ECHOED. A FIGURE EMERGED
FROM THE DARKNESS—THE MIRROR DEMON. ITS EYES GLOWED RED, AND
IT CARRIED AN AURA OF MENACE.

"WELCOME TO MY DOMAIN, MONK," THE DEMON SNEERED. "HERE, EVERYONE MUST FACE THEIR DEEPEST FEARS. LET US SEE HOW BRAVE YOU TRULY ARE."

KAI STOOD FIRM. "I WILL NOT BE SWAYED BY FEAR," HE SAID. THE DEMON
WAVED A CLAWED HAND, AND THE SHADOWS AROUND HIM BEGAN TO SHIFT.

SUDDENLY, KAI WAS STANDING ON A HIGH, CRUMBLING BRIDGE OVER A RAGING RIVER. HE FELT HIS HEART RACE. HEIGHTS HAD ALWAYS UNSETTLED HIM.

THE DEMON'S VOICE TAUNTED, "CAN YOU CONQUER YOUR FEAR, MONK? OR
WILL YOU FALL LIKE THE OTHERS?"

TAKING A DEEP BREATH, KAI CALMED HIS MIND. HE FOCUSED ON THE SOUND OF THE RIVER, GROUNDING HIMSELF. STEP BY STEP, HE CROSSED THE BRIDGE.

WHEN HE REACHED THE OTHER SIDE, THE ILLUSION DISSOLVED. THE DEMON'S FACE TWISTED IN FRUSTRATION. "IMPRESSIVE. BUT LET'S SEE HOW YOU FARE NEXT!"

THIS TIME, KAI FOUND HIMSELF IN A BURNING LIBRARY. FLAMES ROARED AROUND HIM, AND PRECIOUS SCROLLS—KNOWLEDGE HE CHERISHED—TURNED TO ASH.

"YOUR FEAR OF LOSING WHAT YOU VALUE MOST," THE DEMON
CACKLED. "WATCH IT ALL DISAPPEAR."

KAI CLOSED HIS EYES AND REMINDED HIMSELF, "KNOWLEDGE LIVES WITHIN US, NOT JUST IN BOOKS." WITH THAT THOUGHT, THE FLAMES DIED DOWN, AND THE LIBRARY VANISHED.

THE VILLAGERS, STILL TRAPPED, BEGAN TO HOPE. "BROTHER KAI IS STRONG," THEY WHISPERED. "PERHAPS HE CAN SAVE US."

BUT THE MIRROR DEMON WAS NOT FINISHED. "YOUR GREATEST FEAR IS YET TO COME," IT HISSED, AND THE SHADOWS SWIRLED AGAIN.

KAI STOOD IN A SILENT MONASTERY. HE SAW HIS YOUNGER SELF, SURROUNDED BY ANGRY FACES. MEMORIES OF A MISTAKE HE'D MADE AS A NOVICE MONK RESURFACED.

THE DEMON WHISPERED, "GUILT—YOUR HEAVIEST BURDEN. RELIVE IT, MONK." THE
SCENE REPLAYED, EACH WORD CUTTING DEEPER.

KAI TOOK A DEEP BREATH. "I HAVE MADE PEACE WITH MY PAST. I HAVE
LEARNED AND GROWN FROM IT." THE SCENE MELTED AWAY, AND THE
DEMON SHRIEKED IN RAGE.

THE SHADOWS AROUND THE VILLAGERS BEGAN TO LIFT. THEIR FEARS WEAKENED AS KAI'S COURAGE STRENGTHENED.

"YOU CANNOT WIN," THE DEMON GROWLED, GROWING LARGER AND MORE TERRIFYING. "I AM FEAR ITSELF!"

KAI STEPPED FORWARD, UNDAUNTED. "FEAR ONLY HAS POWER WHEN WE LET IT. YOU HAVE NO HOLD OVER ME."

THE DEMON LUNGED, BUT KAI HELD UP A SMALL, POLISHED MIRROR HE HAD CARRIED WITH HIM. THE DEMON FROZE, SEEING ITS REFLECTION.

THE MIRROR GLOWED BRIGHTLY. THE DEMON WRITHED AND SHRANK, ITS POWER REFLECTED BACK UPON ITSELF. "NO!" IT SCREAMED, BEFORE VANISHING INTO NOTHINGNESS.

THE SHADOWY WORLD DISSOLVED, AND KAI AND THE VILLAGERS FOUND
THEMSELVES BACK IN THE FOREST, THE CURSED MIRROR
SHATTERED AT THEIR FEET.

THE VILLAGERS CHEERED AND EMBRACED EACH OTHER. "YOU SAVED US, BROTHER KAI!" THEY EXCLAIMED. "HOW CAN WE EVER THANK YOU?"

KAI SMILED GENTLY. "FEAR CAN BE DEFEATED WITH COURAGE AND UNDERSTANDING. REMEMBER THIS, AND YOU WILL BE FREE FROM ITS GRIP."

THE VILLAGERS CARRIED THE SHARDS OF THE MIRROR BACK TO THE MONASTERY, WHERE THEY BURIED THEM DEEP BENEATH THE EARTH.

FROM THAT DAY FORWARD, THEY SHARED THE STORY OF BROTHER KAI'S
BRAVERY, TEACHING GENERATIONS TO CONFRONT THEIR FEARS.

KAI CONTINUED HIS PEACEFUL LIFE, HELPING OTHERS AND SPREADING WISDOM WHEREVER HE WENT.

IN THE EVENINGS, HE WOULD MEDITATE BY THE MOUNTAINSIDE, REFLECTING ON HIS JOURNEY AND THE LESSONS LEARNED.

HE UNDERSTOOD THAT FEAR WAS A PART OF LIFE, BUT IT COULD BE
OVERCOME WITH INNER STRENGTH AND CLARITY.

AS THE SEASONS PASSED, THE FOREST WHERE THE MIRROR HAD ONCE STOOD GREW LUSH AND VIBRANT AGAIN, FREE OF ITS DARK CURSE.

THE VILLAGERS OFTEN VISITED KAI TO SEEK HIS GUIDANCE, INSPIRED BY HIS UNSHAKABLE SPIRIT.

THE MONK'S TALE TRAVELED FAR AND WIDE, INSPIRING EVEN THOSE
WHO HAD NEVER MET HIM.

AND THOUGH KAI'S ADVENTURE WAS OVER, HE KNEW HIS PURPOSE
REMAINED—TO HELP OTHERS FACE THEIR OWN FEARS.

FOR AS LONG AS COURAGE SHINES BRIGHTER THAN FEAR, NO DARKNESS
CAN EVER TRULY WIN.